Six Great Piano Trios

Opp. 1, 70 and 97

by Ludwig van Beethoven

DOVER PUBLICATIONS, INC., NEW YORK

Published in Canada by General Publishing Company, Ltd., 30 Lesmill Road, Don Mills, Toronto, Ontario.
Published in the United Kingdom by Constable and Company, Ltd.

This Dover edition, first published in 1987, is an unabridged republication of Nos. 79 through 84 of Series 11 ("Trios für Pianoforte, Violine und Violoncell") of the collection *Ludwig van Beethoven's Werke; Vollständige kritisch durchgesehene überall berechtigte Ausgabe. Mit Genehmigung aller Originalverleger,* originally published by Breitkopf & Härtel, Leipzig, n.d. [1862-65].

The publisher gratefully acknowledges the cooperation of the Paul Klapper Library, Queens College, for the loan of the music reproduced in this volume.

Manufactured in the United States of America
Dover Publications, Inc., 31 East 2nd Street, Mineola, N.Y. 11501

Library of Congress Cataloging-in-Publication Data
Beethoven, Ludwig van, 1770-1827.
  [Trios, piano, strings, Selections]
  Six great piano trios.

  Reprint. Originally published: Leipzig : Breitkopf & Härtel, 1862-1865. Originally published in series : Ludwig van Beethoven's Werke.
  Contents: In E-flat major, op. 1, no. 1—In G major, op. 1, no. 2—In C minor, op. 1, no. 3—[etc.]
  1. Piano trios—Scores. I. Beethoven, Ludwig van, 1770-1827. Trios, piano, strings, op. 1. 1987. II. Beethoven, Ludwig van, 1770-1827. Trios, piano, strings, op. 70. 1987. III. Beethoven, Ludwig van, 1770-1827. Trios, piano, strings, op. 97, B♭ major. 1987. IV. Title. V. Title: 6 great piano trios. VI. Title: Great piano trios.
M312.B42 1987   87-750046
ISBN 0-486-25398-8

Contents

Trio in E-flat Major for Violin, Cello, and Piano, Op. 1, No. 1   1
(composed ca. 1793; dedicated to Prince Carl von Lichnowsky)

ALLEGRO, 1.   ADAGIO CANTABILE, 11.   SCHERZO. ALLEGRO ASSAI, 16.   FINALE. PRESTO, 19.

Trio in G Major for Violin, Cello, and Piano, Op. 1, No. 2   31
(composed 1794–1795; dedicated to Prince Carl von Lichnowsky)

ADAGIO/ALLEGRO VIVACE, 31.   LARGO CON ESPRESSIONE, 45.   SCHERZO. ALLEGRO, 52.
FINALE. PRESTO, 54.

Trio in C Minor for Violin, Cello, and Piano, Op. 1, No. 3   67
(composed 1794–1795; dedicated to Prince Carl von Lichnowsky)

ALLEGRO CON BRIO, 67.   ANDANTE CANTABILE CON VARIAZIONI, 76.
MENUETTO. QUASI ALLEGRO, 82.   FINALE. PRESTISSIMO, 84.

Trio in D Major for Violin, Cello, and Piano, Op. 70, No. 1 ("Ghost")   95
(composed 1808; dedicated to Countess Marie von Erdödy)

ALLEGRO VIVACE E CON BRIO, 95.   LARGO ASSAI ED ESPRESSIVO, 103.   PRESTO, 111.

Trio in E-flat Major for Violin, Cello, and Piano, Op. 70, No. 2   121
(composed 1808; dedicated to Countess Marie von Erdödy)

POCO SOSTENUTO/ALLEGRO MA NON TROPPO, 121.   ALLEGRETTO, 131.
ALLEGRETTO MA NON TROPPO, 138.   FINALE. ALLEGRO, 145.

Trio in B-flat Major for Violin, Cello, and Piano, Op. 97 ("Archduke")   157
(composed 1810–1811; dedicated to Archduke Rudolph)

ALLEGRO MODERATO, 157.   SCHERZO. ALLEGRO, 169.
ANDANTE CANTABILE MA PERÒ CON MOTO, 179.   ALLEGRO MODERATO, 190.

Trio in E-flat Major

Op. 1, No. 1

1

SCHERZO.
Allegro assai.

Trio in G Major

Op. 1, No. 2

attacca subito il Allegro.

Allegro vivace.

SCHERZO.
Allegro.

Trio in C Minor

Op. 1, No. 3

MENUETTO.
Quasi Allegro.

FINALE.
Prestissimo.

Trio in D Major
Op. 70, No. 1 ("Ghost")

98 • Trio in D Major, Op. 70, No. 1 ("Ghost")

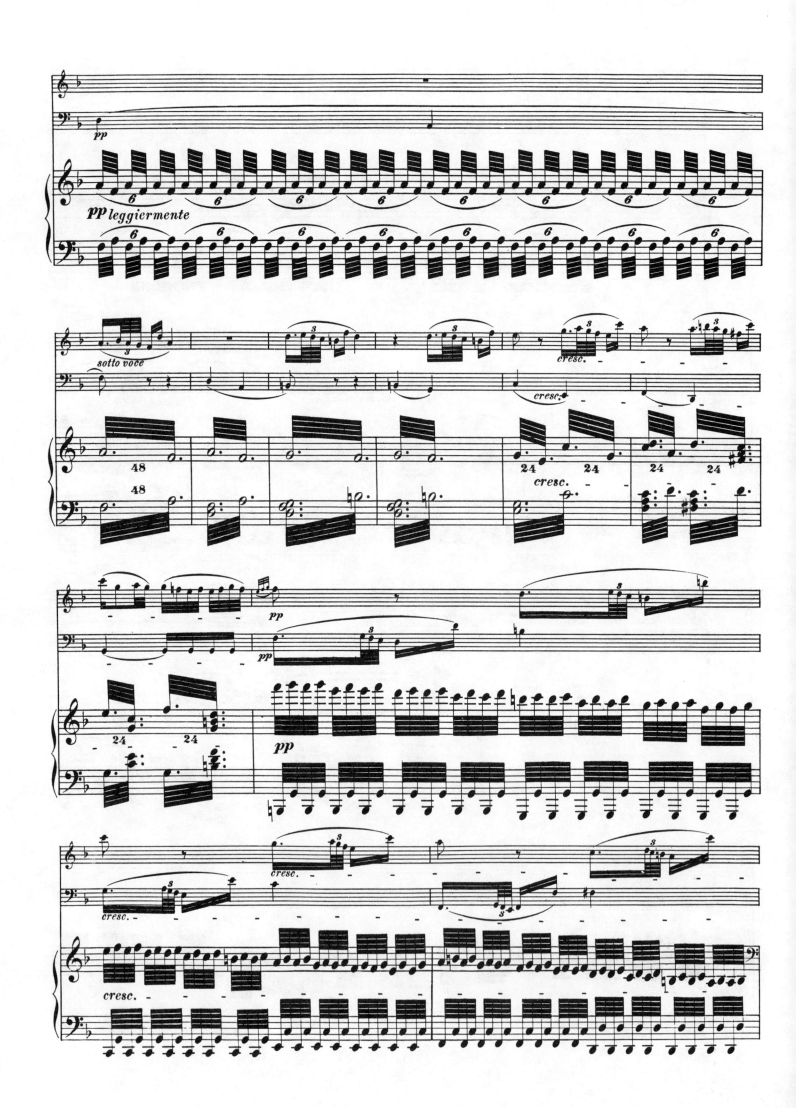

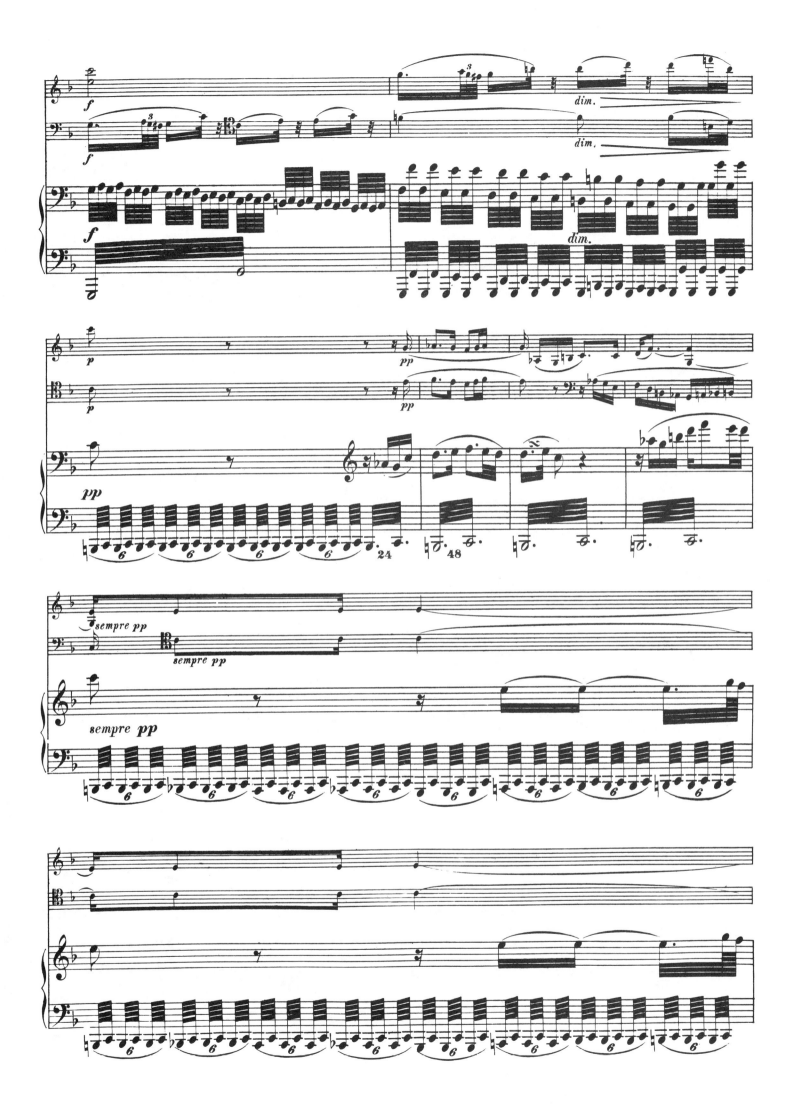

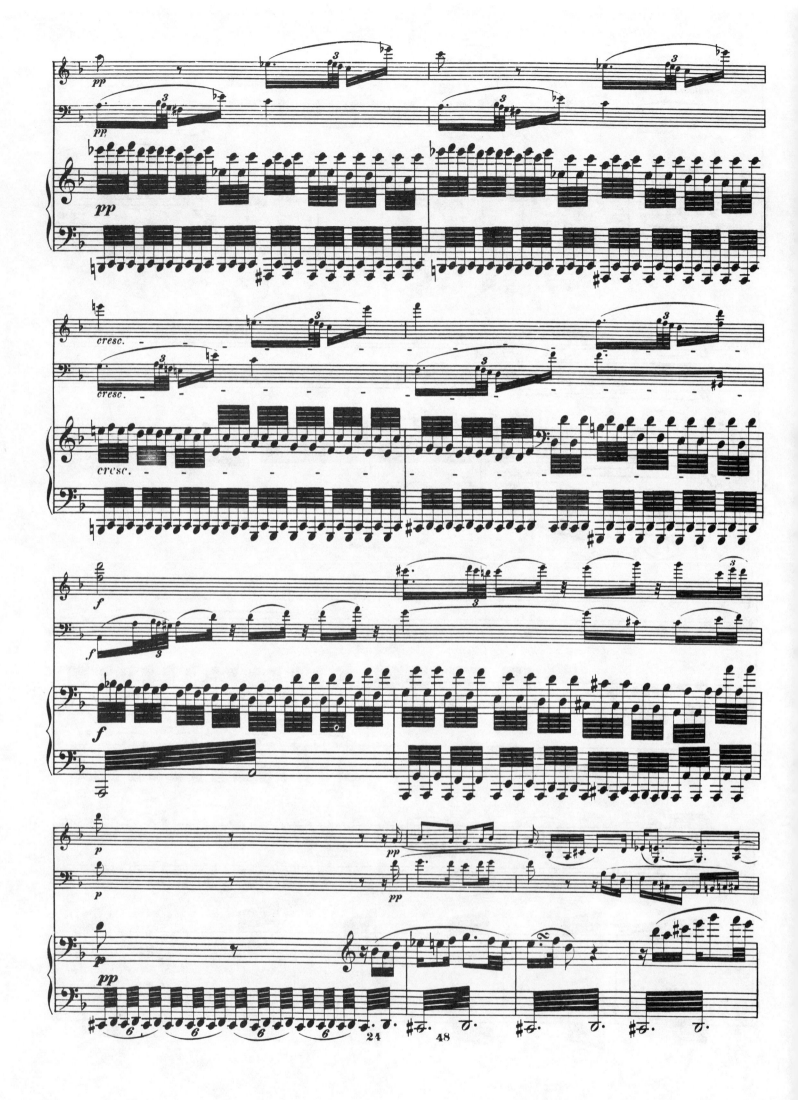

108 • Trio in D Major, Op. 70, No. 1 ("Ghost")

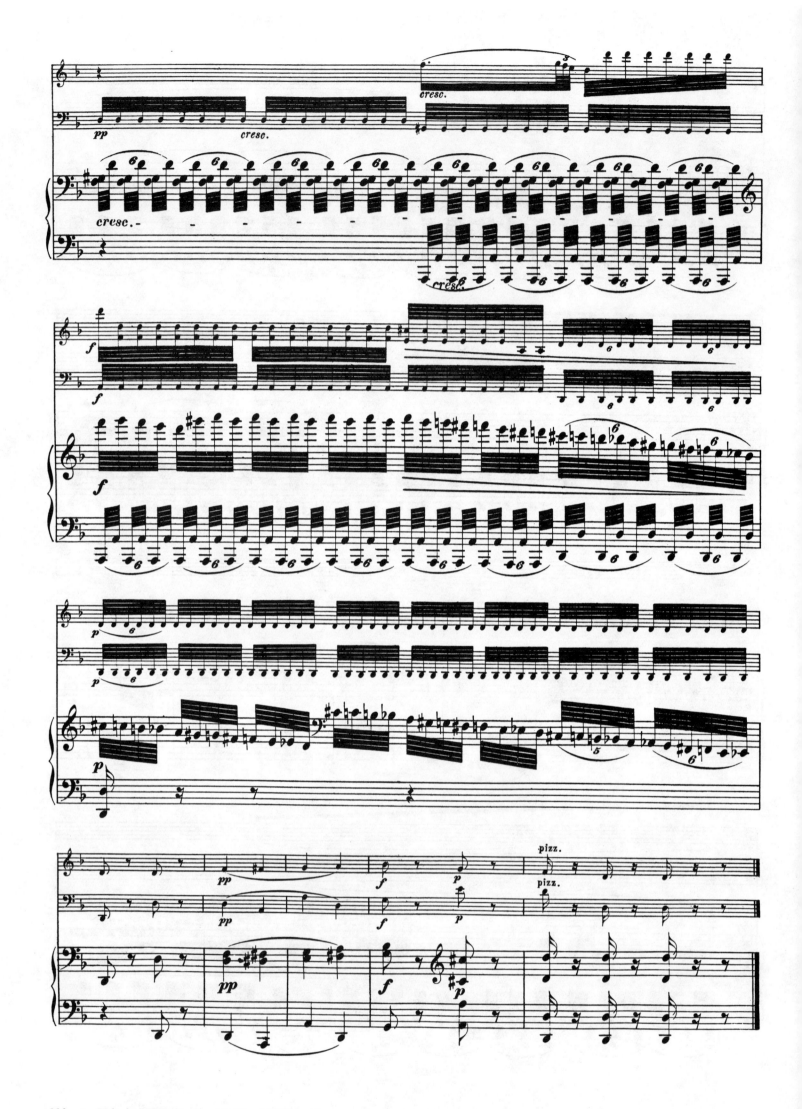

Trio in E-flat Major

Op. 70, No. 2

FINALE.
Allegro.

Trio in B-flat Major
Op. 97 ("Archduke")

SCHERZO.

Allegro.

190 • Trio in B-flat Major, Op. 97 ("Archduke")

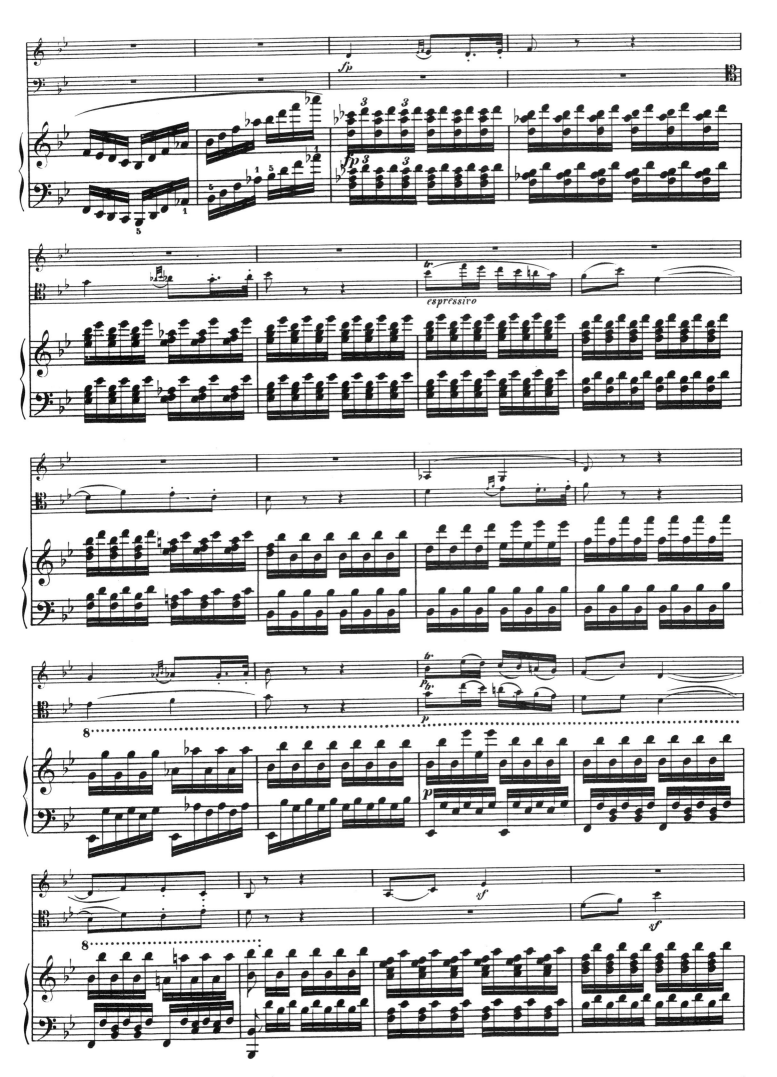